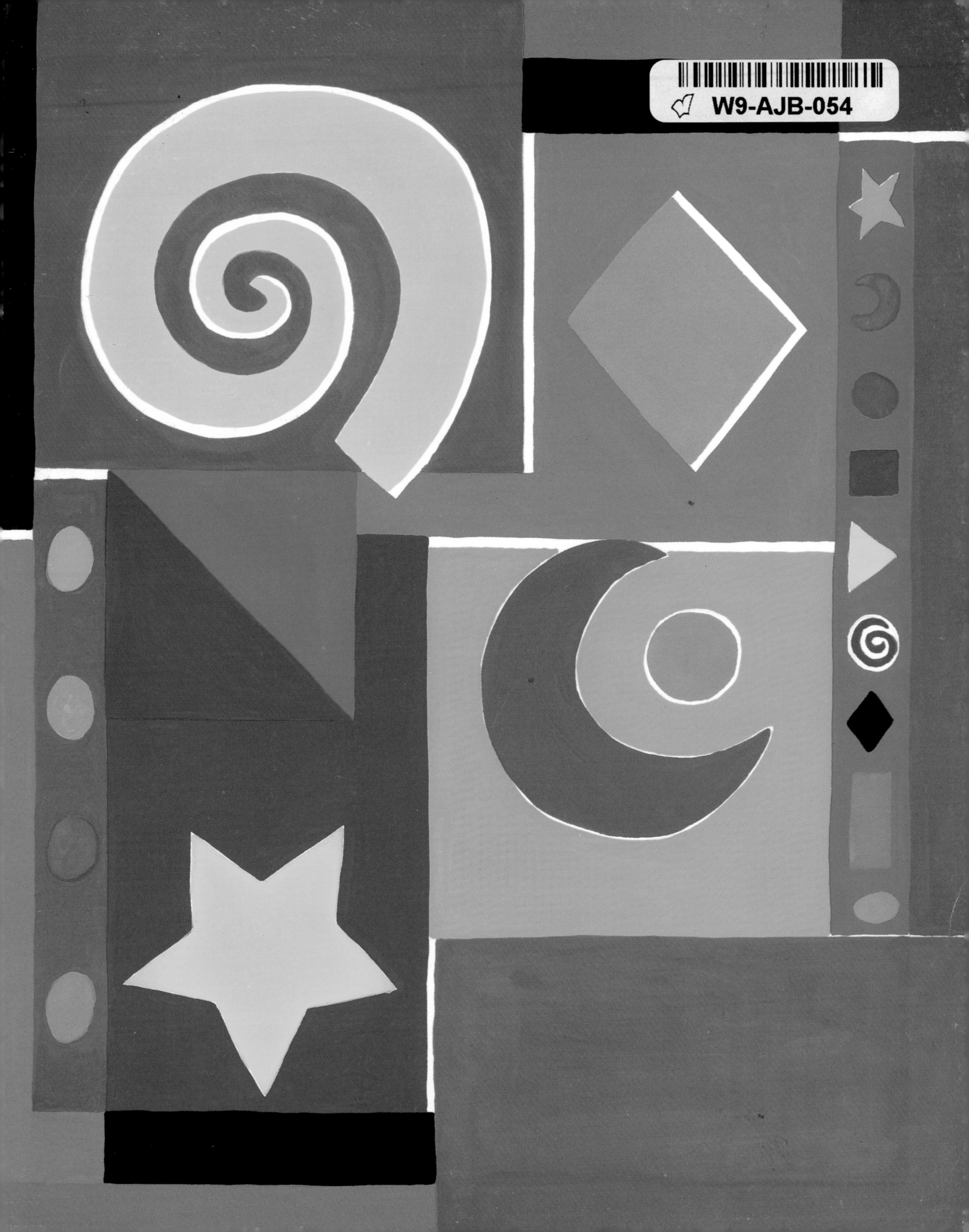

THE SHAPES GAME

PICTURES BY
SIAN TUCKER

VERSE BY
PAUL ROGERS

Henry Holt and Company
New York

Also by Paul Rogers

FROM ME TO YOU
WHAT WILL THE WEATHER BE LIKE TODAY?

For Judith Elliott
P.R.

To Jann and Tony
from Sian

Text copyright © 1989 by Paul Rogers
Illustrations copyright © 1989 by Sian Tucker
All rights reserved, including the right to reproduce
this book or portions thereof in any form.
First published in the United States in 1990 by
Henry Holt and Company, Inc., 115 West 18th Street,
New York, New York 10011.
Originally published in Great Britain in 1989 by Orchard Books,
96 Leonard Street, London EC2A 4RH.

Library of Congress Cataloging-in-Publication Data
Rogers, Paul
     The shapes game,
     Summary: Basic shapes are introduced through a
simple riddle verse.
     1. Geometry—Juvenile literature.   [1. Shape.
2. Geometry]   I. Tucker, Sian, ill.   II. Title.
QA445.5.R64   1990   516'.15   89–19957
ISBN 0–8050–1280–X

Henry Holt books are available at special discounts
for bulk purchases for sales promotions, premiums,
fund-raising, or educational use. Special editions
or book excerpts can also be created to specification.
For details contact: Special Sales Director, Henry Holt and
Company, Inc., 115 West 18th Street, New York, New York 10011.

First American edition
Printed in Belgium

10 9 8 7 6 5 4 3 2 1

Shapes all around us.

Shall we play a game?

I'll spy a shape —

You say its name!

I spy a bubble,

A bouncy round ball,

A wheel shape, a sun shape,

A bang-the-big-bass-drum shape —

The shapes you see are all . . .

circles

I spy a steeple,

A gleaming Christmas tree,

A sail shape, a cone shape,

A little-pile-of-stones shape —

What shape can you see?

triangles

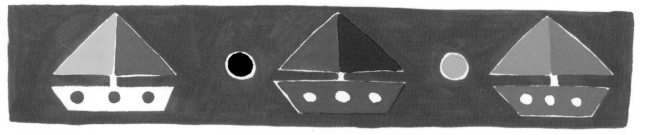

I spy a handkerchief,

A patch on someone's dress,

A tile shape, a dice shape,

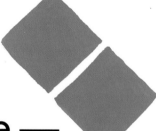

A clinking-chunk-of-ice shape —

All are more or less . . .

s q u a r e

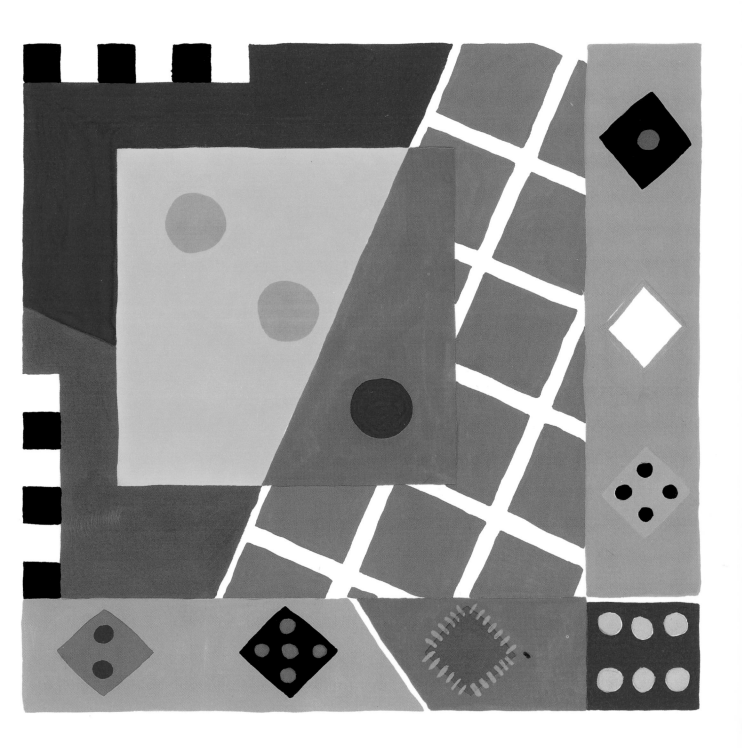

I spy a snowflake,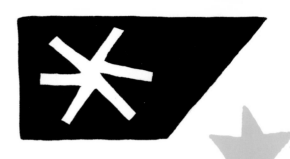

The flashing of a gem,

A flower shape, a spark shape,

A twinkle-in-the-dark shape —

What's the word for them?

s t a r s

I spy a bird's egg,

Leaves on the trees,

A prune shape, balloon shape,

A face-seen-in-a-spoon shape —

What are all of these?

o v a l s

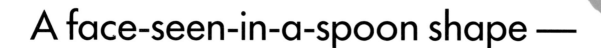

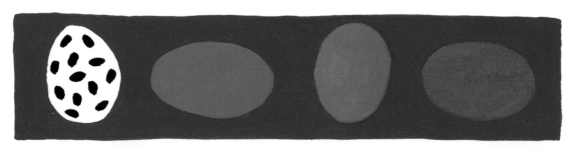

I spy a hammock,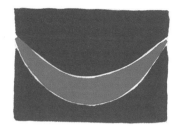

A slice of melon rind,

A smile shape, a skipping shape,

A fingernail-clipping shape —

Every one a kind of . . .

crescent

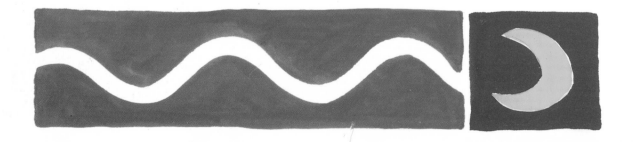

I spy a doorway,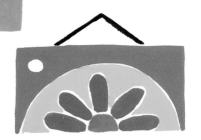

A picture on the wall,

A window shape, a cage shape,

A look! — this-very-page shape —

These shapes we call . . .

rectangles

I spy a snail shell,

A twist of curly hair,

A drill shape, a screw shape,

A twirling-the-lasso shape —

Name the shapes there.

spirals

I spy a bright kite

Dancing on the breeze,

A bird's-open-beak shape,

A not-allowed-to-peek shape —

What's the word for these?

d i a m o n d s

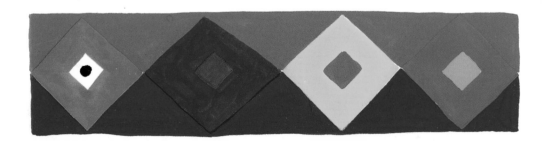

I spy a diamond,

A crescent and a star,

A spiral, circle, triangle,

An oval, square and rectangle —

Show me where they are.

Shapes on the ceiling,

No two the same —

Quick — before they disappear —

Give them all a name!